Wendell Phillips Garrison

The Benson Family of Newport, Rhode Island

Together With an Appendix Concerning the Benson families in America of

English Descent

Wendell Phillips Garrison

The Benson Family of Newport, Rhode Island
Together With an Appendix Concerning the Benson families in America of English Descent

ISBN/EAN: 9783744728805

Printed in Europe, USA, Canada, Australia, Japan

Cover: Foto ©ninafisch / pixelio.de

More available books at **www.hansebooks.com**

THE

BENSON FAMILY

OF

Newport, Rhode Island.

TOGETHER WITH AN APPENDIX CONCERNING THE

BENSON FAMILIES IN AMERICA

OF

English Descent.

PRIVATELY PRINTED.

New York: The Nation Press.

—

DECEMBER, 1872.

NIL SINE BONUM

Copies of this book have been deposited in the following libraries:

BENSON FAMILY OF NEWPORT.

RÉSUMÉ.

The following outline will serve to gather up the lines of descent elaborated above. It includes only the head, of families whose lives have been treated of at length :

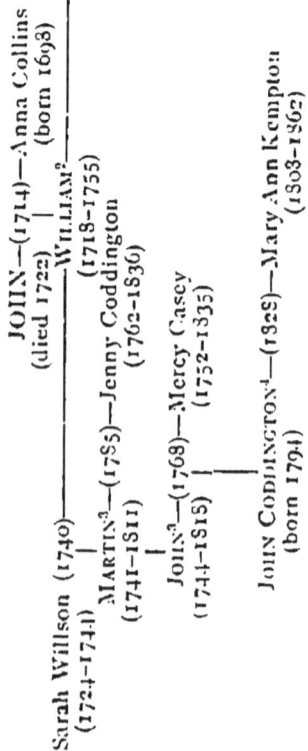

JOHN—(1714)—Anna Collins
(died 1722)   (born 1698)

WILLIAM[2]————————————(1745) Frances Gardner
(1718–1755)   (1724–1773)

Sarah Willson (1740)
(1724–1741)

MARTIN[3]—(1785)—Jenny Coddington
(1741–1811)   (1762–1836)

JOHN[3]—(1768)—Mercy Casey
(1744–1815)   (1752–1835)

JOHN CODDINGTON[4]—(1829)—Mary Ann Kempton
(born 1794)   (1803–1862)

GEORGE[3]—(1793)—Sally Thurber
(1752–1836)   (1770–1844)

GEORGE WILLIAM[4]—(1833)—Catherine Knapp Stetson
(born 1803)   (born 1809)

ADDENDA.

Page 14. GARDINER BENSON. "Late of Newport," says the mention of his death in the Providence *Gazette :* from which it may be inferred that his life was chiefly spent in his native place.

Page 19. Capt. MARTIN BENSON. The exact date of his marriage was August 28, 1785. (Trinity Church Records.)

Page 43. In addition to the anti-slavery societies herein named, similar organizations existed in Maryland (1789), Connecticut (1790), Virginia (1791), New Jersey and Delaware (1792). The New York Society was organized Jan. 25, 1785, and Alexander Hamilton succeeded John Jay as President. (See the interesting paper by Mr. William F. Poole, of the Cincinnati Public Library, published in the Cincinnati *Gazette* of Nov. 28, 1872, "Sketch of Anti-Slavery Opinions before the Year 1800.")

" HAPPY is the people whose history is not long." The Newport Bensons share this felicity. The public records of them suffered in common with those of the town in consequence of the British occupation, and the dispersion caused by this event and by other circumstances peculiar to the family resulted in the almost total destruction of their private papers. The last depositary of these was the Rev. °John³ Benson, who had in his possession at the time of his death his father's and grandfather's books of account, bills of lading and of sale, and other documents which in all probability would have thrown light on their English connections. He had also written out with great pains a full autobiography, but he died before he could publish it, and we have in place of it the very meagre account of his seven voyages described hereafter (p. 23). The family papers stored away in his desk were left by his son in Pomfret, Conn., as was supposed in trustworthy hands, but they were wantonly destroyed. There remained only traditions too vague and fleeting for even the best of memories, and which in the line of °George³ Benson had wholly faded, leaving nothing certain except that Newport was the cradle of the family. The venerable representative, almost the oldest survivor, to whom I have dedicated the fruits of my enquiries, retained more of the knowledge necessary to such an undertaking as this than any of his relatives. He at least furnished the clues, which I had only to follow up.

The shortness and uncertainties of life are my excuse for committing this genealogy to press in the imperfect state in which it is. I feel that I have satisfied all reasonable curiosity as to their lineage on the part of the descendants of John¹ Benson, without much calling conjecture to my aid, and never, I trust, unjustifiably. Whenever it was possible to refer to any authority I have done so, and this will not only neutralize any errors there may be in my transcription, but enable others, if they see fit, to extend my researches.* This is particularly true of the Appendix, in which I have felt it my duty to gather all the information which I have acquired incidentally concerning other Benson families in America, omitting those of Dutch descent.

If the fewness of the Newport Bensons has rendered my task more difficult by exposing their records to the fate which I have described as having overtaken them, it has, on the other hand, permitted me to clothe the usual skeleton of a genealogy with something like real flesh, without transcending the limits which a natural regard for his pocket ever imposes upon the antiquary not more blessed with means than with leisure. I have brought out as far as was discreet the character and idiosyncrasies of each subject in turn, and have here and there preserved some trait of the times or the place which may serve to give life and reality to the picture.† Had

---

* For this purpose I will here note that I have looked pretty carefully through the Boston *News-Letter* for the years 1704-1742, inclusive ; 1755-1770, inclusive ; 1780 and 1783. Providence *Gazette*, 1762-1767, inclusive ; 1771 : 1777-1787, inclusive ; and 1791-1796, inclusive. Newport *Mercury*, 1762-1767, inclusive. My impression is that I have looked much further among these old files (not always complete, by the way), but have omitted to keep an account of them. The Newport correspondence of the *News-Letter* was of great service to me, and I regret I have not had time to examine the same in the contemporary press of New York. The advertisements were also highly serviceable.

† The temptation to do much more of this than I really allowed myself was almost overpowering, and I was constantly on the search for an appropriate place in which to stow away such items as these :

—James Codine arrived at Newport " last Lord's Day " (Feb. 22, Boston *News-Letter*, Mar. 2, 1719) in 17 hours' passage from New York—"the like never known before, and bound there again."

—The Episcopal Church was first established in Rhode Island (Newport) in 1704.

—Trinity Church spire, Newport, blown down in the great gale of Oct. 23, 1761 (*News-Letter*, Oct. 29) ; raised by 45 Sons of Liberty, July 18, 1768 (*Ib.* July 28).

—By the census of 1774, Providence had 655 families, 4321 inhabitants. (As for Newport, see p. 16.)

I been seconded in this (particularly in dealing with the fourth generation), I should not now be obliged to apologize for what seems like partiality or negligence in the compiler. The same cause has prevented me from carrying out my intention of illustrating this genealogy with photographs.

The *focus* of the Benson tribe in America was in the district lying between Massachusetts and Narragansett Bays; but, though they almost elbowed each other from Hull to Newport, I have not discovered any connection between the Old Colony and Aquidneck families. Neither the North Burying Ground on Thames Street, nor the Clifton Burying Ground at the head of William and Tower Streets, has revealed the resting-place of the founder; but even without the date of his birth I believe it can be positively asserted that his name does not occur among those recorded in the Appendix.

Nothing was pleasanter in the whole of my experience of what I must call a fascinating pursuit than the uniform courtesy I met with from utter strangers, and the great pains often taken to facilitate my researches. To make my acknowledgments is therefore a duty of the most agreeable sort; and passing by my relatives and their ever cordial co-operation, I must express my deep indebtedness from first to last—and at the last almost as much as at first—to Dr. Henry E. Turner, of Newport, whose kindness has far exceeded any claim I could have upon him, and whose laborious gleanings from old records and papers have saved me years of blind groping, and given its chief value to my account of the first two generations. If I could make such a return for his unselfish assistance as I should like, it would be to ensure the publication in a permanent form of the vast amount of genealogical data which he has collected in the spare hours of a busy professional life.* Next after him I must mention

* This would be a graceful recognition of Dr. Turner's services if undertaken by the Rhode Island Historical Society; and I would also direct to it the attention of the New England Historic-Genealogical Society of Boston.

Mr. Joseph M. Hammett, of Newport, who most obligingly volunteered to search the graveyards for me, and whose success furnished me with some important particulars not elsewhere obtainable. Mr. N. H. Gould will also accept my thanks for many favors, along with Messrs. Benjamin Marsh, 2d, and William G. and David Stevens, all of Newport. In Providence I received substantial aid from Messrs. J. Carter Brown (uncle and nephew), and from Hon. J. R. Bartlett, late Secretary of State; and more or less of interest or friendly attention has been shown me by the Rev. David Benedict of Pawtucket, the late Rev. S. J. May of Syracuse, Mr. Benson J. Lossing of Dover, N. Y., Messrs. William H. Whitmore and Albert H. Hoyt of Boston, and Mr. William Still of Philadelphia. To all these gentlemen, to Dr. N. B. Shurtleff of Boston, to Mr. Reuben H. Guild, librarian of Brown University, and to the librarians and other officers of the Redwood Library, the Rhode Island Historical Society, the Massachusetts Historical Society, the New England Historic-Genealogical Society, the New York Historical Society, and the New York Genealogical and Biographical Society, I tender my grateful acknowledgments.

W. P. G.

New York, November 1, 1872.

THE BENSON FAMILY

OF

NEWPORT, RHODE ISLAND.

𝔍𝔬𝔥𝔫 𝔅𝔢𝔫𝔰𝔬𝔫, as appears from the records of
Trinity Church, Newport, was married, October
11, 1714, to Anna Collins,* who figures in the
town records as the administrator of her late
husband, under date of August 6, 1722. This is
all that is positively known in regard to him,
and it is even a matter of inference that he is the
founder, though of this there can be little doubt
—first, because in the later generations but one
line of Bensons is found in Newport; and,
second, because William ² Benson was baptized
in Trinity Church, and named one of his sons
William Collins, as will be seen hereafter. That
John Benson came to this country after May,
1692, may be conceded from the fact that he is
not included in Savage's Dictionary. That he
was a ship-owner or captain is probable from the

---

* Probably the first child of William Collins and Sarah Whitman, born January 29,
1698.

fact that commerce was the occupation of the family to the third generation, both William[2] and Martin[3] bearing the title of Captain. And finally, it seems altogether likely that he is the same John Benson who "cleared outwards for Rhode Island"[*] from Boston in December, 1719 (*News-Letter*, Dec. 21), and arrived some time before the New Year (*ib.* Jan. 4, 1720); who was announced to sail on his return trip "with the first opportunity" (*ib.* Feb. 15), and arrived duly in Boston in the ship *Ann*[†] (*ib.* Mar. 14). No other trace of him, it is believed, occurs in the *News-Letter* during the years 1718-1722. The most thorough search in the graveyards of Newport has failed to discover any monument of him.

Tradition assigns him three sons: one, who removed to North Carolina, probably at the time of a somewhat general migration from Newport to that colony, in which the Eastons were prominent, though they afterwards worked up into Virginia (near Richmond) and Pennsylvania, and are believed to have intermarried with the Bensons. Mrs. Martin[2] Benson, in her latter years, forwarded a miniature of her deceased son, Martin[4], to relatives (presumably Bensons) in Virginia. Another son is reported to have settled in Savannah, Georgia, and become a planter. This one, it is related, was often visited by his nephew, Captain Martin[3] Benson.

The first of these was presumably

I. i. JOHN HENDRICK,[‡] or JOHN BENSON, JUNIOR. At least it

seems proper to identify the two. The records of Jamestown, near Newport (April 5, 1736), show that John Benson, junior, was married to Anne Crocum, (qu. Slocum ?—
a Jamestown name), December 9th [1735]. From the record
of the Second Congregational Church, Newport (and also
from the town records), it appears that John Hendrick
Benson was married June 13, 1745, to Ann Hinkley. Sup-
posing both to be one and the same person, he is in all
probability the North Carolina colonist and ancestor of
JOHN BENSON, JUNIOR, of Columbia, Penn., who married Abigail Shearman, daughter of Samuel, of Portsmouth, near
Newport, February 26, 1824 (Newport *Mercury*, Feb. 28),
but concerning whom enquiry has failed to discover any-
thing further.

2. ii. WILLIAM, baptized August 29, 1718 ; died July 19, 1755.
3. iii. (If tradition is insisted on, the family order might, con-
sistently with the dates, stand thus : i. John, jr. ; ii. William ; iii. John Hendrick.   But it would seem odd that the
name of John should be twice bestowed upon living children in the same family.)

SECOND GENERATION.

William² Benson, according to the records of
Trinity Church, was baptized August 29, 1718,
but from the inscription on his tombstone it may
be gathered that he was born some months previous to that date. He was admitted a freeman
of the Colony by the General Assembly at Newport, May 1, 1744 (Bartlett's "Rhode Island
Colonial Records," vol. v., p. 81). The trade of
Newport with Africa direct had sprung up while
he was yet a lad,* and he succeeded to it not un-

---

* In the Boston *News-Letter* of Nov. 25, 1725, may be found what is believed to be
the first mention of it. The Newport Custom-house announces (Nov. 13) the departure
of Jonathan Thurston "for Affrica," and (Sept. 16, 1726—*News-Letter*, Sept. 22) his return
from Guinea ; the next year, Wm. Barry, for Africa (Jan. 21, 1726—*News-Letter*, Jan. 27).
Hitherto Newport's commerce had been chiefly with the South and the West Indies. The
commerce of the colony at the date of Capt. Benson's marriage is well depicted in the following extracts from the Report of Governor Richard Ward, on paper money, to the Rt.
Hon. the Lords and Commissioners of Trade for the Foreign Plantations, Newport, Jan.
9, 1740 (Bartlett, vol. v., p. 13) :

"We have now about 120 sail of vessels belonging to the inhabitants of this colony,
all constantly employed in trade, some on the coast of Africa, others in the neighboring
colonies, many in the West Indies, and a few in Europe.   .   .   .   .   .

"In short, if this colony be in any respect happy or flourishing, it is paper money, and
a right application of it, that hath rendered us so. And that we are in a flourishing condition is evident from our trade, which is greater in proportion to the dimensions of our
government than that of any colony in Her Majesty's American Dominions.

"Nor have we served ourselves only by engaging so deeply in navigation. The
neighboring governments have been in a great measure supplied with rum, sugar, molasses, and other West India goods by us brought home and sold to them here. Nay,
Boston itself, the metropolis of the Massachusetts, is not a little obliged to us for rum and
sugar and molasses, which they distil into rum, for the use of their fishermen, etc.

"The West Indies have likewise reaped great advantage from our trade, by being
supplied with lumber of all sorts, suitable for building houses, sugar-works, and making
casks ; beef, pork, flour, and other provisions, we are daily carrying to them, with horses
to turn their mills, and vessels for their own use ; and our African trade often furnishes
them with slaves for their plantations. To all this, we beg leave to add that the mer-

naturally if the son of a sea-captain and a merchant. He is said to have had three ships devoted exclusively to fetching cargoes of golddust, ivory, and slaves. He died of a consumptive disorder July 19, 1755, "in the 38th year of his age," and was buried in the old North Cemetery, where his grave is still marked (along the path leading to, and near, the southern entrance).

He was twice married: first, to Sarah Willson*—according to the town records [June] 5, 1739, and if so, during a violent outbreak of small-pox in Newport; but probably June 5, 1740 (Trinity Church), when his townsmen, and possibly he among them, had had nearly a year of very successful privateering against the Spaniards, not a Rhode Island vessel having been lost, and the spoils having undoubtedly been great. By this wife he had:

4. i. MARTIN, born October 2, 1741; died December 24, 1811.

ii. WILLIAM COLLINS, born January 30, 1742-3; died ——.

5. iii. JOHN, born June 20, 1744; died December 28, 1818.

His second wife was Frances, daughter of Deputy-Governor John Gardner† and his wife

chants of Great Britain have, within these twelve months, or thereabouts, received seven or eight sail of ships from this colony for goods imported here of late, and sold to the inhabitants."

  * Born about 1724, died December 23, 1744, in the 20th year of her age, six months after the birth of her youngest child. She was probably the daughter of Jonathan Willson (gentleman) and Hannah his wife; the former died September 2, 1729, in his 31st year. His grave is the third to the north of his daughter's, which stands beside her husband's.

  † He was Assistant to the Hon. John Wanton, Esq., Governor, in 1736, and on Mon-

Frances * (Sanford). They were married October 3, 1745. By her he had two sons:

iv.   GARDINER, born August 15, 1747; died in Providence, between two and three o'clock on Sunday morning, January 24, 1796. His death, from consumption, was preceded by three weeks of very painful confinement, in which he was faithfully attended by his younger brother George, who was greatly attached to him, his half brother John, then a Baptist clergyman, and also by the Rev. Dr. Gano, of the same denomination. George wrote of his last hours:

"I expressed to him my regret that he had not come in town before his disorder had acquired an incurable ascendency. He replied: 'Don't reflect, don't reflect; these things are all ordered, wisely ordered.' It may be remarked that his cough was extremely troublesome, and such his debility of body that he has at times coughed perhaps ten minutes before he could expectorate ; and so excessively emaciated that it produced a sore in his back distressing to those who beheld it. Yet he assured me that his light afflictions were nothing, though he said, ' No tongue can tell what I suffer. I endeavor,' he added, ' to put on patience.' My Aunt Wanton,† who attended in his chamber the four weeks preceding his death, declares that ' he never uttered a complaint, nor even an impatient expression'; on the contrary, appeared thankful for the least attention to him, and often expressed much apprehension that he gave his friends too much trouble. He had lived a regular and moral life, and for several months previous to his confinement employed a great part of his time in reading the Bible and other religious books."

His remains lie buried in the North Burial-ground, in Providence. On the tombstone is inscribed: "His moral character was blameless, but his hope was in Christ."

6. v.   GEORGE, born August 20, 1752; died December 11, 1836.

---

day, May 3, 1758, was elected Deputy to the Hon. Stephen Hopkins, Governor. He was born, of Joseph and Catharine (Holmes) Gardner, September 17, 1697, and died January 20, 1774.

* Daughter of John Sanford and his wife Frances (Clarke), daughter of Jeremiah² Clarke, son of Governor Jeremiah Clarke. Mrs. Benson's tombstone, beside her husband's, bears the following inscription: " In memory of Frances, relict of William Benson, Merchant, and daughter of the Hon. John Gardner, Esq. She died November 30, 1773, in the 47th year of her age."

† Probably Elizabeth Gardner, who married Captain Peter Wanton.

THIRD GENERATION.

Martin [3] **Benson** was born in Newport, October
2, 1741. At the time of his father's death, he
had probably received some training in the business of a foreign merchant, even if he had not
already made a voyage or two as supercargo.
He continued the African trade upon which his
father had entered, and resided for a number of
years on the coast of Africa. Of the dates of
his movements we have no record, and can only
conjecture that it was he who was met by his
brother John in London in the year 1759–60.
He was for some time Governor of the Island of Goree,* and when he returned home
brought with him a large property, his bottled
gold-dust alone (according to the family tradition) requiring two wheelbarrow loads to
transfer it from the ship to the shore. He
purchased what was then and still is known
as the Governor Wanton House,† on the west

---

* This island, of considerable importance in the palmy days of the slave trade, has
had a romantic history, not easy to gather from any single source. It was ceded to the
Dutch in 1617 by King Biran of Cape Verd, and by them fortified. They were driven out
in 1663 by the English Admiral Holmes, but recovered Goree under De Ruyter in 1665,
only to lose it finally in 1677, when attacked by a French squadron under Count d'Estrées
—a conquest confirmed to France in the following year by the treaty of Nimeguen. The
English retook the island in 1759, and relinquished it by the treaty of 1763 ; again captured it in 1773, and held it till 1784. In 1804 they reoccupied it, and in 1814 restored it to
France, whose possession it has ever since been. For a map of the island, see Golberry's
"Fragmens d'un Voyage en Afrique, fait pendant les années 1785, 1786, 1787 " (Paris,
1802).

† Originally Governor William, afterwards his son, Governor Joseph, Wanton's.

side of Thames Street (present numbers 85–89), one of the finest residences in town, with a commanding prospect across the Bay, where he lived for many years and brought up his family. Besides this house, he is reputed to have owned* the Long Wharf or dock which is the present landing for steamboats from New York. He was also the owner of other real estate.

The date of Captain Benson's return is quite obscure, though it may be inferred that it was after 1774, as the census of Newport for that year does not contain the name of Benson. Possibly he arrived immediately after the evacuation of the town by the British (Oct. 25, 1779).† That he was at home early in 1780, appears from the proceedings of the General Assembly at Newport on the second Monday of September of that year (Bartlett, vol. ix., p. 230):

The former was Governor in 1732, and died in 1733. The latter was Governor from 1769 to 1775, and died July 17, 1780, his wife Mary having died March 2, 1767. (See the Providence *Gazette* of March 14, 1767, and July 29, 1780; and Boston *Gazette* of July 31, 1780).

* There is some doubt about this. In March, 1764 (see the Newport *Mercury*), the wharf was sold to the highest bidder; and in April, 1795, it still appeared to be public property, as there was a lottery to build a hotel and public school, and to repair the wharf.

† The beginning of the British occupation was in December, 1776, and at its close the town had been more than half deserted. (By the census of 1774, Newport had a population of 1,590 families, or 9,208 persons.) The State House was left in ruins, and more than 500 buildings had been destroyed. The Jews, who especially contributed to the prosperity of the place, had departed to Providence, Leicester, and Boston. To such a state were the inhabitants reduced, that contributions were forwarded from Boston and other neighborhoods to relieve their distress. The British "carried with them the records of the town from its settlement [in 1638]. The vessel containing these precious papers was sunk at Hell Gate. Three years afterwards the half-obliterated fragments were returned to the town, and a copy was made of such portions as were still legible" (Arnold's "History of Rhode Island," vol. ii., p. 448).

"Whereas, Mr. Martin Benson, of Newport, preferred a petition, and represented unto this Assembly, that in May last he obtained permission from the council of war of this State to proceed to the island of St. Christopher's for the purpose of recovering his property, then in the said island ; that, in pursuance of said permission, he took passage in the sloop *Hope*, Captain Benjamin Alger, bound to Grenada ; that the said sloop was taken in the passage, and carried into Antigua, where he procured a vessel, which he manned with Americans, and proceeded to St. Martin's, and from thence to St. Christopher's, where he recovered his property, and took the same on board ; that in order to secure his vessel from being captured by British vessels-of-war, he obtained a clearance for Halifax, in Nova Scotia, with an intention to put into the first port he should make within the United States ; that in the prosecution of his said intention, he was taken by the ship *Rhodes*, Nehemiah Buffington, commander, belonging to Salem ; that, notwithstanding he produced the resolve of the council of war as aforesaid, and the permission of his Excellency the Gover-nor grounded thereon, his vessel and papers were taken from him, and sent into Salem ; and thereupon prayed this Assembly to grant him letters recommendatory to the Legis-lature of the State of Massachusetts, that he may obtain satisfaction for the injury he has received—which, being duly considered,

"'It is voted and resolved, that the said petition be, and the same is hereby, granted ; that William Channing and Thomas Rumreill, Esquires, be, and they are hereby, appointed a committee to draught a letter accordingly ; and that they report the same as soon as may be.'"

No other trace of this appears on the records, nor is it known if the attempt went further than the petition. The files of the Boston papers of that date, however, show that if any attempt was made it was fruitless. In the Boston *Gazette* of July 31, 1780, it is reported that "Saturday

last a prize Snow * laden with English goods
arrived at Salem." In the same paper of September 11 and 18, we find the libel, to be tried
in Maritime Court, Boston, October 3, 1780, of
" Nehemiah Buffington, commander of the armed
ship *Rhodes*, against the brig *Susannah*, burthen
100 tuns, or thereabouts, William Bryant [or
Bryans], late master." The *Gazette* of Monday,
November 27, contains this advertisement: " To
be sold at the North Bridge in Salem, on Thurs-
day, the 30th of November, inst., . . also,
the brig *Susannah*, about 80 tuns burthen."

An unhappy domestic occurrence about the
year 1808 broke up Mr. Benson's household,
and darkened the remainder of his days. Accompanied by his son, John Coddington, he
made a voyage to the coast of Africa, before
reaching which they were becalmed for several
days, and suffered greatly from want of water,
until relieved by a passing vessel. A severe attack of gout—a disease to which Mr. Benson
was subject—superinduced by the privations of
the voyage, ended in his death. The event is
briefly recorded in the Newport *Mercury* of
February 22, 1812, and as follows in the Providence *Gazette* of February 15:

"At Goree (an island on the coast of Africa), on the
24th of December last, Captain Martin Benson, late of Newport, in this State, aged 71 years. This respectable, enter-

* * *Snow*—a vessel with two masts resembling the main and foremasts of a ship, and
a third small mast just abaft the mainmast, carrying a sail similar to a ship's mizzen "
(Mar. Dict.). A sort of hermaphrodite brig.

prising gentleman commenced his mercantile career with very flattering prospects, and, for some time, fortune smiled on his honest, animated efforts; but in the course of his variegated life, ill health, and a series of disasters, which prudence could not avert nor caution escape, unhappily interposed to blast his anticipated comforts—his fairest expectations. Yet he did not despond, but virtuously pursued the even 'tenor of his way,' respected and beloved, till Death closed this transitory scene, and removed him to another and, we trust, 'a better world.'

" . . . 'Death is victory;
'It binds in chains the raging ills of life.'

"His remains were very respectfully entombed on the day following, attended by the Governor and officers of the British garrison at Goree, with a number of private gentlemen."

Captain Benson was a man of fine personal appearance and of many accomplishments; affable and courteous, and much esteemed by the ladies, who called him their walking-staff. He had long been regarded as an old bachelor when the following announcement appeared in the Providence *Gazette* of September 3, 1785: "Married, at Newport, Mr. Martin Benson, merchant, to Miss Jenny Coddington,* daughter of the late Captain John Coddington." This lady's parents were married January 28, 1759, and it is probable that she was born about 1762–63, which would make her more than twenty years younger than her husband—a disparity too great for happiness, as the sequel proved. Mrs. Ben-

---

* Her mother was Mary, daughter of Governor Joseph Wanton, and died at Newport, Sunday evening, February 4, 1793, in her 65th year (*Mercury*, February 13). Captain John ⁴ Coddington was the son of William³, or Nathaniel³, sons of Nathaniel², the second son of Governor William Coddington. He was lost at sea in 1762.

son, who is still remembered by many citizens of
Newport as a very dignified old lady, died
December 6, 1836 (*Mercury*, Dec. 10; but the
age assigned her is certainly excessive). The
circumstance of her sending a miniature of her
son Martin to relatives in Virginia has been
already mentioned. The children of this marriage were :*

7. i. MARTIN, born probably in 1786. He was educated at
Brown University, and graduated in 1806, his chum being
the late Hon. John H. Clarke, formerly United State Sena-
tor from Rhode Island, and one of his classmates being the
Rev. David Benedict, well known as the author of a History of the Baptists, and still living. Young Benson chose
law for his profession, and is said to have established himself in New York, though the name is not found in the di-
rectories of that city. On learning of the death of his
youngest brother, he resolved to visit Sierra Leone with
the same object ; and, having provided himself with the
necessary documents, embarked (1816 ?) in a vessel which
sailed from New York, and was never heard of afterwards.
He was married in the spring of 1811 to Amey Smith, at
North Providence (Providence *Gazette* and Newport *Mercury* of June 1, and *Rhode Island American* of May 31). The
officiating clergyman was the Rev. Ferdinand Ellis, Con-
gregationalist, who died in 1858. The *Gazette's* notice ob-
scurely reads : "Mr. Martin Benson (S. J.)"

ii. WILLIAM COLLINS. All that is known of him, except
that he died of consumption, and was buried in Governor
Wanton's tomb, is contained in these two obituary notices :
From the Newport *Mercury*, October 8, 1803 :

"On Sunday, the 25th ult., William Benson, son of Mr. Martin
Benson, of this town, in the sixteenth year of his age. This was an
amiable and promising young man. He had just completed an

* There is said to have been a beautiful daughter Ann (named after Ann Wanton ?),
who was buried in the Wanton tomb. This tomb, by the pious care of Mr. Nathan
Gould, is now marked in the Clifton burying-ground by a substantial marble stone, inscribed : "The Family Tomb of Governor Joseph Wanton."

education adapted to the course of life he had chosen for his pursuit. A happy fancy gilded the prospect before him, and with the warm heart of youth he was hastening to enjoy it."

From the Providence *Gazette* of the same date :

"Master William Benson, son of Martin Benson, Esq., in his 16th year. He was, by his amiable manners, endeared to all who knew him, and his dawn of life seemed to promise future excellence."

iii. JOHN CODDINGTON, born in Newport in the first days of November, 1794. He was educated for the navy. Before his studies were completed, his father took him with him (1811 ?) to West Africa, and, as already related, he shared the hardships of the voyage which proved fatal to the former. He was, on the death of his father, invested with his African estate, but appears to have returned home immediately, and the outbreak of war with England hastened his entrance into the United States Navy, which was favored by Commodore Perry's intimacy with the family. He was (Cooper's "Naval History") commissioned midshipman August 22, 1812, and probably was assigned at once to the United States ship *Adams*, 42 guns, Captain Charles Morris, which sailed from the Chesapeake in January, 1813, passed to the south of Bermuda, crossed the Atlantic, captured a number of prizes (the last of which, the India ship *Woodbridge*, taken on the 25th of March, had to be abandoned), and arrived home in April (p. 243, "Naval Monument," Boston, 1836). The tradition is that he was with Perry on his flagship at the battle of Lake Erie, September 10, 1813 (but this lacks confirmation). He was certainly on the *Adams* when, on September 2, 1814, as it lay at Hampden on the Penobscot, having just returned from a cruise, it was surprised by a large British fleet with troops, and blown up by Captain Morris to avoid its falling into the enemy's hands. (*Ib.* pp. 248, 249.) The crew escaped to land, and dispersed in the woods between the Penobscot and the Kennebec, rendezvousing at Portsmouth. They were then transferred to the *Congress*, 36 guns, lying at Boston, under the same commander as before. But peace was declared before the vessel was ready for sea. The "Naval Register" for 1815, in which Mr. Benson appeared as midshipman, shows that he was furloughed June 19, 1815. Desirous of disposing of his father's estate in Africa, he got a situation as first mate of the brig *Caroline*, Captain Jenckes, lying at Providence, and bound for Martinique and Sierra Leone. After being three days at sea, the brig was capsized in a storm, washing overboard the captain and cabin-boy. Mr. Benson, thus being left in command, as soon as the storm abated, ordered one of the crew to dive down and unloose the lashed helm, and again another, but both were afraid to venture. He himself then dived, and was never seen again.

John³ Benson was born in Newport, June 20, 1744. His life was more checkered than any recorded in this genealogy, and he left behind him a very minute and voluminous account of it, of which the original MS. has been unfortunately lost. A condensed account of his voyages was published (prior to 1824) by his youngest son, making a small volume, with the following title : "A Short Account | of the | Voyages, Travels, and Adventures | of John Benson ; | comprising | Seven Voyages | to different parts of the World; | interspersed | with | Anecdotes and Observations | upon | Men and Manners. | *Written by himself.* | '*Omne tulit punctum, qui miscuit utile dulci.*' | Published by John C. Benson. | [*Copyright secured.*]" The compiler, however, gave only the sequence of the voyages, and left the dates, and often the duration of them, undetermined. There is even a discrepancy in the narrative itself, which renders the date of the first voyage doubtful. On the death of his father, in 1755, he was left, at the age of eleven, in charge of his grandfather (*i.e.*, his step-mother's father, the Hon. John Gardner, Deputy Governor), and applied himself diligently to his studies until, as he says (p. 9), "he had arrived at the age of fifteen years, when a strong inclination to travel the seas and visit distant shores" took possession of him. On p. 83, however, he says: "I would inform the reader, that in the *thirteenth* year of my age I attempted a voyage to sea." The first statement is more likely to be the true one, and we may suppose that it was in the summer of 1759 that he was disappointed in getting passage, as engaged, on the "good snow" *Defiance*, Captain Edward Wanton, bound for Africa; but actually sailed a few weeks later in the *Industry*, Captain Edward Emerson, bound for England. This vessel was caught by a French privateer, *Le Triomphe*, in the British Channel, but, except that he was robbed of everything, young Benson fared well, by being taken into the Captain's cabin, till landed with other prisoners at Brest. Here he was for some time detained in prison, but was exchanged in the autumn at St. Malo, and, via Portsmouth, reached London, where he met "a brother" (Martin?), but did not join him. He returned home in the spring on the brig *Osprey*, Captain Thomas Rodman,* of Rhode Island, working his passage, which occupied 72 days. The round trip, including his stay on French soil, consumed 11 months (1759–60). The second voyage was undertaken, "after having remained

---

* This commander subsequently (1765) died on the coast of Africa. (See Newport correspondence. Dec. 30, 1765, in the Boston *News-Letter* of Jan. 9, 1766.)

some time at home," on the *Othello*, Captain Edward Chapman (Messrs. Godfrey and John Malbone owners), which mounted 10 carriage guns and a few swivels, and was bound for Antigua with lumber and provisions. A French privateer easily captured the vessel, through the cowardice of its captain, and Mr. Benson was imprisoned "some time in a gloomy dungeon" in Martinique. Then exchanged and sent to Guadaloupe, he sailed from the latter island in the *Benevolence*, of New Haven, Captain Thomas Rice, via St. Christopher's and Turk's Island to Fisher's Island, opposite Stonington, Conn., whence he made his way back to Newport. All this might have been accomplished in 1760. These two voyages had brought only loss to Mr. Benson, and he sought to repair his fortune on the third, in the *Lydia*, Captain Peter Wanton,* bound for Jamaica. They came back safely with sugars, and the profit answered his expectations. They were pursued by a large ship of war, but escaped. This voyage should probably be assigned to 1761. The fourth voyage, which he entered upon "forthwith," was in the *Rising Sun*, of Newport, Captain William Pinnegar, mounting 10 carriage guns and 8 swivels—a capture from the French. Her destination was Barbadoes, the bay of Honduras, and Holland. In 30 days they reached Barbadoes, and sold

---

* Probably his kinsman, who married his step-mother's sister, Elizabeth Gardner.

4

their cargo for slaves, cash, and rum, and Mr. Benson notes that he saw there, "at high-water mark, the heads of slaves, fixed upon sharp-pointed stakes, while their unburied carcases were exposed to be torn by dogs and vultures on the sandy beach." They could not gain access to Honduras Bay, as it was blockaded, but anchored a league from Musquito Inlet, where, in a December hurricane (1761), the ship was run on shore, and, out of a company of 25 (it is not clear whether this included the poor slaves), 16 were lost, among them a kinsman (Conkling) of Mr. Benson. He himself, although carrying a lame arm in a sling, managed to reach the shore, and to walk to the British garrison at Black River, where the survivors were humanely received by the governor, Mr. Pitt. Capt. Pinnegar saved enough from the wreck to purchase a smaller vessel, in which Mr. Benson sailed to Jamaica, and three weeks later worked his passage thence to Newport in Captain Gregory Cozzens's ship (early in 1762). Still undaunted, "after a few weeks' respite on shore," he embarked on the schooner *Polly*, Captain Peter Wanton, for Africa. They made for Sierra Leone, and thence to Anamaboe, where they bought 90 slaves, and then set sail for Guadaloupe, where, not finding a market for their human merchandise, they kept on to Monte Christi, and sold to the Spaniards. They had been absent eleven months when they returned to Newport (1763). Another slave-trading venture of the same Captain Wanton, in the *Charming Abigail*, tempted Mr. Benson to ship under him after he had "become tired of loitering on shore." But he nearly lost his life when they had been but a short time at sea, by falling overboard as he was endeavoring "to throw the fore-topsail out of the netting." He swam out of the ship's way, and, catching a rope, was saved. They were obliged to put back to Newport on account of a rotten mast, and were two months in reaching Sierra Leone. Twenty miles up the river they took in slaves and rice to feed them with, and then sailed to the Gold Coast* and Anamaboe. This was a rendezvous for slavers, and here they found a Philadelphia ship, Captain William Rodman of Rhode Island, together with a Rhode Island ship, Captain James Searing. The slaves that Rodman had on board rose, and their example was followed on Wanton's vessel, where, however, the timely warning of a "Dunko" negro saved the crew. When the slaves came to be sold at Guadaloupe, for sugar, this faithful black was disposed of along with the rest. "I blush to record so in-

---

* The Providence *Gazette* of Feb. 25, 1764, announces the arrival upon the Coast of Captains Earl, Carpenter, Edward Wanton, Peter Wanton, and Gardner, from Rhode Island. Captain Edward Wanton left the Coast in February (see Boston *News-Letter* of July 5), and returned home without his ship in June (see *News-Letter* of June 28), and reported Captains *Wanton*, Woodbury, and Morris, from Newport, as being still on the Coast at the time of his departure.

famous a deed," says the autobiography. Captain Searing died of an epidemic that prevailed among the shipping, and Mr. Benson was near sharing the same fate. He lay for so long in a trance that he was thought to be dead, and perhaps with any other captain than a kinsman would have been committed to the deep. While in this condition, he experienced a vision which he relates at length in his narrative, and which changed completely his views as to the sinfulness of slave-trading, as well as awakened his religious nature with startling power. Capt. Wanton arrived with his cargo of slaves at St. Kitts early in 1765 (Providence *Gazette* of Feb. 16, and Boston *News-Letter* of Feb. 21). Shortly after his return, Mr. Benson retired to Warren, about 18 miles from Newport, intending to quit the life of a seafarer, which had been so disastrous to him ; but at the end of three years and a half (1768 ?) he resolved on a short voyage to North Carolina, and shipped in the *Enterprise*, Captain John Bush, for that purpose, with a cargo of naval stores. By falling overboard from a boat, and encountering a fearful storm while crossing the Gulf Stream, his life was twice imperilled in this trip ; and if he had been born to be drowned, a speedy opportunity offered when he was upset in crossing the harbor of Stonington. He was rescued from the eel-grass which abounds on those shallows by the singular and, as he re-

garded it, Providential agency of a floating board
with a crooked nail which caught in his shoulder.
Having received a good education, including a knowledge of Latin, he engaged in
teaching, and, after he had received a call to the
Baptist ministry, he continued to teach as well as
to preach in various places, and at length, about
1804, settled in Pomfret, Connecticut, where he
died of pleurisy December 28, 1818, leaving a
widow and seven children.

Mr. Benson was an accomplished accountant
and penman, but he resisted the persuasion of
friends to engage in business rather than enter
the ministry.   He was a fine reader and singer.
It was probably in 1768 that he married Mercy,
daughter of John Casey, who owned some 1,200
acres in South Kingston, R. I., on what is called
Boston Neck.   She was born April 28, 1752,
and was a woman of unusual mental and physical powers—her strength in lifting, indeed, being something incredible in these days.   She
was an excellent manager of household affairs,
making up for her husband's deficiency in that
respect.   After his decease, she lived with her
youngest son till her death, which happened
July 22, 1835, when she was buried beside Mr.
Benson, in the family burying-ground at Pomfret,
a handsome monument marking their common
grave.   They had in all ten children, as follows :

i. SALLY, born January 4, 1769; died November 24, 1837. She married Amos Boyden, of Mendon, Mass. They had David, Joel, and William ; and daughters Abigail (?), born about 1790, and married ; Nancy, unmarried ; Amy, married (?) ; and one who became the wife of a Mr. Taft. In all, seven children.

ii. NANCY, born May 28, 1771 ; died June 25, 1845. She married John Amidon, of Douglas, Mass. They had Samuel, William, and John ; Celinda, who married Abijah Easty ; and perhaps other daughters.

iii. POLLY, born June 10, 1776, and still living, the oldest descendant of John[1] Benson. She married Stephen Kempton, of Mendon, Mass. They had Martin, Millens, and Harrison ; and four daughters.

iv. MARTIN, born 177– ; died of croup at the age of three.

v. MARTIN, born 17— ; died young.

8. vi. MARTIN GARDINER, born March 14, 1781 ; died February 6, 1859. He was bred a mechanic, and was a man of good physical and mental capacity. He was married and had children, of whom two sons survived him.

vii. FANNY, born March 20, 1783; died March 20, 1862. She married James Mitchell.

viii. BETSEY, born November 6, 1788 ; died January 2, 1816. She married Sterry Angell, of Pomfret, Conn.

9. ix. WILLIAM COLLINS, born March 9, 1791 ; died June 10, 1858. He was settled as a farmer in the northern part of New York, where he reared a large family whom he left in comfortable circumstances. Having been called to Paterson, N. J., to attend his sick brother, he died and was there buried in his brother's lot. A stone marks his grave.

10. x. JOHN CODDINGTON, born November 3, 1794.

George³ Benson was born in Newport, August
20, 1752.* Concerning his early youth and
training his descendants have no knowledge or
tradition. He was, as he says in one of his letters, "left fatherless so early as to have no recollection of a single feature in his countenance";
and, in another, he laments "his want of a
liberal education," though he was a very correct
writer and a handsome penman. He had come
to Providence and engaged as clerk with Nicholas Brown & Co.,† merchants, as early as 1771.
Three years later,‡ he was in doubt whether to

* The town records say 1751.
† Consisting of Messrs. Nicholas, Joseph, and Moses Brown. Nicholas died June
4, 1791; Moses in September, 1836, three months before Mr. Benson himself.
‡ NEWPORT April 4th, 1774.
SIRS: I have Consulted my Friends on the subject of my continuing at Providence
or Returning to abide in this Town, and have attentively Considered the matter myself.
There is very engaging motives to Invite my Return here, as I have repeatedly ob-
served, But Considering the Peculiar State of your Business (Tho, I don't mean entirely
to exclude Self Interest, that, I own, has a Share in the Proposal) have Concluded, that
if its *agreeable*, and you will add Thirty Dollars more a year to my Present Terms,
will engage again in your Employ, But should not Chuse to Contract for any Certain
Time, tho, you may Rely I will not Leave your Business without Due notice, and expect to Continue with you (should my Proposal Suit) untill next Fall *at Least* at which
Time, its Probable I may engage with my uncle Wanton, if his Business *should succeed
according to his wishes.*—I Purpose to return to Providence this Week, but Should be
Glad of your Reply as soon as may be, that I may adjust Matters here, accordingly.
In the mean Time, or Rather at all Times,
I am your Assured Friend,
GEORGE BENSON.
Mr. M B's. Letter to his Friend Willson I Left in
the Drawer as Capt. Grinnell does not expect to sail
untill next Sunday. I saw A Johnson in the Street, he
told me he wrote you a few Days Past—is it True—or was it only to Prevent a Dunn—
Would it not be a Good Time to have some Paper added to the Ledger. It will be
needed soon, let who will be Clerk.

remain in Providence or to return to Newport,
but was probably granted the modest addition
to his salary which he made a condition of stay-
ing.* The outbreak of the Revolution appears
to have unsettled him. In 1775, he is said to
have ridden on horseback from Providence to
army headquarters at Cambridge, on the mem-
orable 17th of June. In 1779, he was employed
by Col. Ephraim Bowen, Deputy Quartermaster
General,† for how long a period is unknown.
In the spring of 1783, Mr. Benson had removed
to Boston and engaged in partnership with
Joshua Eaton, as appears from the curious document printed in full below,‡ whose strict and

* He had gone to Newport to attend his mother in her last illness. The Newport
Mercury of Dec. 6, 1773, has the following notice : " Last Tuesday died, in the 49th year
of her age, Mrs. Frances Benson, widow of Mr. William Benson, late of this town, deceased, and second daughter of the late Hon. John Gardner, Esq. She was a lady of
great virtue and piety ; a most tender, affectionate parent, and a faithful friend. Her remains were interred on Saturday." (See ante, p. 14.)

† Rhode Island Historical Collections, Book vi. pp. 224, 227. Col. Bowen writes
Gen. Nathanael Greene (then at Middlebrook, Va.), under date of Feb. 8, 1779 : " As Mr.
[George] Olney leaves me to-morrow, I have engaged George Benson to take his place
--Mr. Olney can give you his character. I gave Mr. Olney eighty dollars per month,
and engaged to board him and his wife for that sum, which I did, notwithstanding every-
thing rose 30 per cent. afterwards. Have engaged Mr. Benson at $100 per month till your
pleasure can be known, and, if you do not consent to allow it, I am to lose it, the over-
plus. It is very difficult to get a person to take charge of books and cash that can be entrusted without giving him a price something adequate to the business and the rise of
boarding." Gen. Greene's reply is characteristic (Feb. 23) : " The wages of Mr. Benson
are very high, but you had better give a high price for a good man than employ a bad
one for nothing at all."

‡ " COPPY OF AN AGREEMENT SIGNED BY GB'S TWO APPRENTICES IN BOSTON."

This Agreement Witnesseth, That we John Bryant Junr. and John Crosby, both of
Boston in the County of Suffolk and Commonwealth of Massachusetts minors with the
consent of our respective Parents have entered into the following Engagements with
Messrs. Joshua Eaton & Geo Benson both of Boston aforesaid Merchants, commonly
known by the firm of Eaton & Benson . . . . viz: . . .

1st We Engage faithfully to Keep all the secrets of their Business, to obey all their Law-

onerous requirements the clerk of our day would
stand aghast at. The first advertisement of the
new firm occurs in the Boston *Gazette* of April
7, 1783, and is dated April 3. It enumerates as
"for sale by Eaton & Benson, at their store

full Commands and not to hurt or Injure them or their property or see another do it without Giving them Notice thereof——

2nd We Engage not to risque money or any other Property whatever at Cards, Dice or any other unlawfull Game and that we will not frequent or haunt Alehouses or Taverns, or be from Home unseasonably late at night. . . .

3rd We Promise and Engage in our respective Turns constantly to open and have the Store ready for Business in one hour from Sunrise and never to shut without carefully searching if any Person is in it, and we further Promise to lock the Door securely at one o Clock for Dinner and open it again at three Quarters of an hour past two o Clock in the Afternoon and when it is our respective turns not to open the Store we Engage to be there in one hour from the time fixed for opening in the Morning, and always by three o Clock in the Afternoon——

4th We Engage not to allow any Idle Boys to tarry in the Store on any Pretence whatever, and we will not procure or permit any person not belonging to the Store to assist us in opening of it, making fires, Sweeping &c. . . .

5th We Faithfully Promise and engage to put all the Books (except those usually carried to the House) into the Chest Below every night, and the Cash Books to be accurately compared and made to agree every Evening before the Store is left and that we will not leave in the Store all night any Sum of money exceeding ten Dollars, nor any Note of Hand or any other Valuable Papers whatever. . . .

6th Lastly we Solemnly Promise and Engage to consult the Interests of the said Eaton & Benson in all Cases, to use our utmost Endeavours to secure and protect their property and all other Property whatever that may be comitted to their Care.——

In Witness whereof we have hereto willingly and Cheerfully Set our hands and seals in Boston this twenty Eight day of April, One Thousand Seven hundred & Eighty Three——

Sign'd { John Bryant Junr
J Crosby

Know all Men that we John Bryant & Daniel Crosby both of Boston in the County of Suffolk and Commonwealth of Massachusetts, Fathers to the aforesaid John Bryant Junr & John Crosby, Do hereby Consent to & approve of the Promises and Engagements entered into by our said Sons with the said Eaton & Benson, and we engage to exercise our endeavours & Authority to effect their Complyance therewith & Promise to indemnify & make good to the said Eaton & Benson all damages Sustain'd by Default of our said Sons. In Witness whereof we hereunto Subscribe our Names & affix our Seals this twenty Eighth Day of April One Thousand Seven hundred & Eighty Three.

Sign'd { John Bryant
Daniel Crosby

No. 7 Butler's Row,"* superfine and black pru-
nella, other broadcloths, men's and women's silk
hose, callicoes, linens, Congo tea, green coffee,
ribbons, brown sugars, cotton wools, etc. ; also,
the best James River tobacco. Every month
there was a fresh advertisement; now, "at a
peace price the following articles just received
from Nantz," viz., cutlery, shoe and knee buckles,
etc. ; and now, "by wholesale, at a very low
price indeed," velvets, Marseilles quilting, dia-
per, cogniac brandy, window-glass, pepper,
French and superfine Philadelphia flour, etc.,
etc. On the 18th of August, however, public
announcement was made that the copartnership
had been dissolved on the 12th inst. by mutual
consent, and that Joshua Eaton would "carry
on the commission business as usual" at the old
place. Very likely, offers had been received by
Mr. Benson from Providence which were too
tempting to permit him to stay in Boston longer
than to settle his affairs (the advertisement in
the *Gazette* is inserted for the last time October
27).

In the Providence *Gazette* of January 3, 1784,

---

* So called from Peter Butler, "who figured in Boston about two hundred years
ago, and whose descendants owned the land now bounded by Merchants Row on the
west and by State Street on the south. In 1825 (the time of the great improvement of the
Dock by Mr. Quincy, when the streets parallel to the Market House were laid out),
Chatham street used up Butler's Row, although the name continued to be used many
years after. In 1835, or thereabouts, the opening to the Row was closed by a building ;
so that to-day one can only find the Row by entering a passage-way from State Street.
The old sign *Butler's Row* may be seen in the present building on its south-east corner."
(From a very kind communication by Dr. Nathaniel B. Shurtleff, ex-Mayor of Boston.)

one may see the advertisement of Brown &
Benson, that they have just imported from London, and will sell by wholesale and retail, a general assortment of European goods, etc., "at
their store a little southward of the Great Bridge,
and nearly opposite Nicholas Brown's house."
From this time on, the advertising is constant,
and we may fairly give the credit of it (for it
was very liberal for those days) to Mr. Benson,
seeing what his practice had been in Boston.
Fall and winter goods; flour and European
goods; tobacco and bar-iron; salt in exchange
for fish; West India and New England rum;
flax-seed, etc., etc.—such was the merchandise
of Brown & Benson when, in January, 1791
(see Providence *Gazette* of 22d, etc.), Mr. Nicholas Brown, jr., "being connected in the house,"
the style of it was changed to Browns & Benson,
in whose transactions Russia hemp and duck began to figure prominently. Nicholas Brown, Sr.,
died June 4, 1791,* but the firm was otherwise
unchanged until, on the marriage of Mr. Thomas
P. Ives with Miss Hope Brown (the only daughter of the deceased), March 6, 1792, the only
surviving son and namesake, together with
Messrs. Benson and Ives, "entered into copartnership, and assumed the collection and payment

* Jan. 14, 1791 (Providence Book of Deeds, No. 23, p. 158), "George Benson conveys, by warranty deed, to Nicholas Brown for £250 lawful money, ½ part of a lot of
land on Weybosset St. in Providence, a little southerly from Weybosset Bridge."

of the debts of the late Company,"* and adopted
the style of Brown, Benson & Ives. Their im-
portations now began to spread greatly : wines
from Malaga ; fresh Bohea tea, a great variety
of china-ware, satins, nankeens, lacquered tea-
trays, etc., direct from Canton, in their own ship
John Jay, 460 tons burthen (launched Oct. 8,
1794) ; Swedes-iron ; brandy from Bordeaux ;
and India goods.   June 25, 1796, they offer for
sale their brig *Friendship*, and July 20–August
6, their ship *Hamilton*, just returned from India,
having made a previous voyage or voyages to
Europe.   This latter advertisement is probably
the last put forth by Brown, Benson & Ives.
Mr. Benson withdrew October 17, 1796, being
somewhat fearful of the extended risks he was
called upon to share, and the new firm of Brown
& Ives has remained to this day and acquired a
national reputation.†

Other traces of Mr. Benson as a business man
are to be found in the Providence *Gazette* of
Oct. 6, 1792, from which it appears that on
the Monday previous (Oct. 2), he was unani-
mously elected a director of the Providence
Bank, in place of Mr. Nicholas Brown, who re-
signed in his favor ; and in the same paper of
Jan. 18, 1800, where he figures as director and

---

* Date of March 21, 1792 (Providence *Gazette* of 24th, etc.)

† On this account, it has been thought worth while to preserve the details of its various transformations from the beginning.

secretary of the Washington Insurance Company, of Providence, then just formed. He was also one of the Trustees of Brown University, but retired from the Board in 1801. A letter of his dated September 3, 1801, and addressed to Mr. President Maxcy, is given in Mr. R. A. Guild's " History of Brown University" (Providence, 1867), and is so characteristic as to bear reproducing here :

"Sir :—Will you do me the favor to request the Corporation to accept the following trifling donation for the College Library, viz.: Thoughts on Religion, Natural and Revealed, and Reflexions on the Sources of Incredulity, etc., in 2 volumes, by the Rt. Hon. Duncan Forbes. This is a scarce tho' celebrated performance. A Vindication of the Divine Inspiration of the Holy Scriptures, in answer to Paine's Age of Reason, by Thomas Scott, Chaplain to the Lock Hospital. Discourses on the Genuineness and Authenticity of the New Testament, and on the Nature and Danger of Infidel Philosophy, by the Rev. President Dwight. A Summary of the Evidences of Christianity, by John Fawcett. The Gospel its own Witness, by Andrew Fuller, D.D., to which is subjoined, a Summary of the Principal Evidences for the Truth and Divine Origin of the Christian Revelation, by the Bishop of London.

"May the pernicious errors detected and refuted in the preceding productions be forever excluded from the College, and may the important truths they inculcate and enforce, prevail and abound therein.

"I am, dear sir, assuredly your friend,
"GEORGE BENSON."

Mr. Benson was married Sunday, January 27, 1793, by the celebrated Baptist clergyman Dr.

Stephen Gano, to Sally Thurber,* daughter of
James Thurber (*Gazette*, Feb. 2). They went
to housekeeping (the next year?) in the elegant
residence, near the corner of Angell and Prospect
Streets, which still stands, perfectly preserved
and but little altered. Mr. Benson had built it
for himself in the most thorough manner, and its
site was, in those days, one of the most commanding in the town. Here, in the course of
the next twenty-nine years, all their children
were born. At the end of that time, Mr. Benson, yielding to the solicitations of his son
George, who was very desirous to become a
farmer, let his house, and in the spring of 1824
(the deed bears date Jan. 8) removed with his
family to Brooklyn, Conn. Here he had purchased, though without personal inspection, a
farm of 75 acres, with a substantial house (still
standing), very convenient for his large family.
Possibly he had known something of the locality
on account of his brother John's living in Pomfret close by. There he quietly passed the remainder of his life. "Land," he wrote his son
in 1835 (Oct. 10), "is more secure property
than trade, but for me it is little, very little
profit." He had been a remarkably healthy

* She was born August 28, 1770, and died of consumption in Providence, at the
house of her daughter Charlotte, Sunday, August 25, 1844. Her father (son of Edward[2],
son of James[2], son of John who came to America in 1672) had some time prior to 1768 removed to Durham, Greene Co., New York, where Sarah was probably born. In 1783-4
she was brought to the home of her uncle Edward[4], in Providence, and there brought up.

man, but, having already had a long confinement in 1834 on account of cold, in November
of the following year he contracted another in
Providence which probably never left him, although he seemed to have recovered; and he
died in Brooklyn, on Sunday evening, December
11, 1836, after a painful illness of fourteen days.
It is thought that his life was shortened by leaving off smoking, which had been his habit from
a young man, but which he ceased from at once
when convinced that it was bad. His remains
lie beside those of his wife in the North Burying
Ground, Providence.

Of Mr. Benson's personal appearance some
idea may be had from a miniature painted on
ivory when he was a young man. His skin at
his death was as fair as a child's. He was very
regular and methodical in all his ways, and had
never known, when he died, what toothache or
headache was—all his teeth being sound at
eighty-four. He never ate any supper. His
manners were courtly, and made him a favorite
in ladies' society. In all matters of business he
was very punctilious. It was customary with
him to save every letter, paper, and document
of any interest to himself, and these he carefully
filed way. Especially was he fond of writing
out and communicating to his friends extracts
from moral and religious works, which he likewise preserved. He was at one time a promi-

nent member of the First Baptist Church in
Providence, and as Clerk his name is regularly
affixed to an advertisement in the *Gazette* of
August and September, 1791–4, warning against
"encroachments or nuisances on the Meeting-
house Lot, especially at or near the time of the
annual Commencement" of Rhode Island College. These Commencements were announced
in a companion advertisement, signed George
Benson, Secretary, to be "publicly celebrated
in the Baptist Meeting-house" (*Gazette*, August,
1794–6). It was probably in 1795 that, on oc-
casion of a quarrel between the minister and his
wife, in which his sympathies were with the latter, he withdrew from this church, and never
connected himself with any other, but attended
Friends' meeting mostly. He was by nature
highly philanthropic. As early as 1775, it is
supposed he was interested in the abolition of
slavery in his native State, a letter in the *Gazette*
of Sept. 9, of that year, signed "A Friend of
America," being attributed to him. This communication had reference to a petition to the
General Assembly to pass an act (printed on the
same sheet) "for prohibiting the importation of
negroes into this colony, and asserting the right
of freedom of all those hereafter born or manu-
mitted within the same." At the June session
of the General Assembly, in 1790, was passed an
"Act to incorporate certain Persons by the

Name of The Providence Society for promoting
the Abolition of Slavery, for the Relief of Persons unlawfully held in Bondage, and for improving the Condition of the African Race," of
which the preamble was as follows :

"Whereas a voluntary Society hath subsisted for some
Time past, called *The* Providence *Society for abolishing the
Slave-Trade :* And whereas the Persons hereinafter named,
being Members thereof, have petitioned this General Assembly for a Charter of Incorporation for the said Society,
to enable them more effectually to carry into Execution
the Purposes of their humane Institution, in promoting
the Abolition of the Slave-Trade, and of Slavery, protecting the Rights of Persons unlawfully held in Bondage, and
for improving the Condition of such Blacks as are or may
be emancipated, and of their Posterity :
"SECTION I. *Be it therefore enacted,*" etc.

The list of corporators consisted of 117 persons belonging in Rhode Island, 68 in Massachusetts, 3 in Connecticut, and one in Vermont
—the first New England Anti-Slavery and
Freedmen's Society combined—and was headed
by the Hon. David Howell. The Rev. Dr.
Samuel Hopkins was the thirteenth signer, and
George Benson the thirtieth. The latter was,
as he says, " a member in its very incipient state,
and was one of the first committee appointed to
transact the business during the recess of the
Society"; and, during the closing period of its
existence, was its secretary, as Judge Howell
was its president. This society was evidently
6

patterned after the " Pennsylvania Society for
Promoting the Abolition of Slavery, the Relief
of Free Negroes unlawfully held in Bondage,
and for Improving the Condition of the African
Race," whose first president was Franklin,* and
which voluntarily elected Mr. Benson an honor-
ary member, his diploma bearing date October,
1792. Of the Providence Society, Mr. Benson
further says : " It had the most [more] formida-
ble opposition to encounter than any other.
The inhabitants of Newport had been many
years engaged in that inhuman traffick, which in
its various ramifications furnished employment
to numerous persons. It was the source of almost every other branch of business. Of course
the ship-owners, officers, and seamen, with all
their connections, were inimical to the Society,
as was also the town of Bristol, though of minor
importance. Add to this, some of the principal
merchants in Providence were in the opposition
rank." On Feb. 24, 1834, Mr. Benson was
elected the third president of the New England
Anti-Slavery Society, and served for that year.
When the Windham County (Conn.) Peace
Society was founded in 1826 by the late Rev.

---

* In April, 1787. The Society had been previously organized in 1775 for the pur-
pose of preventing the kidnapping and enslavement of free negroes. A change in the
Constitution took place in. 1787, as indicated in the new title. (See Edward Needles's
" Historical Memoir of the Pennsylvania Society," Philadelphia, 1848.) The New York
Directory for 1786 gives the list of officers of " The Society for promoting the Manumis-
sion of Slaves, and protecting such of them as have been, or may be liberated." The
Hon. John Jay was president.

Samuel J. May, Mr. Benson was probably made president, and, though wishing to resign in 1835, he was continued in the office till his death. He was ever active in distributing documents on "this interesting and truly Gospel subject," as he termed the cause of peace.

Mr. Benson had a crest of arms which he used in sealing his letters. Unfortunately his seal has been lost, but the device is remembered by his son as being identical with that of which a rude cut is here given, from a representation on a piece of family china in the possession of his daughter, Mrs. W. L. Garrison. The seal had a short motto, not exceeding four words, and was attached to the owner's old-fashioned silver watch, which was made in London, and had belonged to his father. Mr. W. H. Whitmore, of Boston, who has been kind enough to examine the crest, expresses his opinion as follows :

"The form of course is heraldic, and though I do not recollect such a crest, I have seen many of a like symbolic nature, e.g., a crowned heart, a dove and branch, etc. It is therefore a possible and not very improbable crest. But I do not find that any English family of the name ever used any crest resembling it. The style of the shield resembles the work of our Callendar, an engraver who made many book plates about 1800 ; and I should suggest that such an origin would be a likely one for this shield. Callendar, like engravers of this date, is *no authority*. He engraved good coats and those without authority indifferently."

As the seal is likely to have accompanied the watch, the origin of the crest must be sought for in a previous generation, especially as Mr. John C. Benson has an independent recollection of its being used by his grandfather, William Benson.

The children of George Benson and Sarah Thurber were as follows :

i. FRANCES, born July 21, 1794; died Oct. 31, 1832, in Brooklyn, Conn., and buried in the North Burying Ground, Providence. Her disease was neuralgia. She was never married.

ii. MARY, born April 24, 1797 ; died in Cambridgeport, Mass., January 29, 1842. Her remains have been deposited in the North Burying Ground, Providence. Her disease was spinal affection. She became a member of the Society of Friends by request, in 1829. She was never married.

iii. SARAH, born January 3, 1799 ; died of cancer, in Northampton, Mass., Sunday, October 6, 1850, and was buried there. She was never married.

iv. ANN ELIZABETH, born October 21, 1801 ; died of dropsy, in Northampton, Mass, September 12, 1843, and was buried there. She was a member of Friends' Society by request. She was never married.

v. CHARLOTTE, born August 3, 1803. Married, October 22, 1826, in Brooklyn, Conn., by Rev. Samuel J. May, to Henry Anthony, of Providence, where they settled and still live. Their children are :

George B., born August 4, died August 18, 1827.——Mary G., born November 13, 1828, and died on the same day.——MARY GOULD, born December 6, 1829 ; married by Rev. E. B. Hall, September 14, 1853, to William C. Townsend, whose children are : Annie, born March 10, 1857 ; Henry Anthony, born September 26, 1860 ; Foster Hodges, born May 15, 1863.——SARAH BENSON, born September 27, 1832 ; married by Rev. Augustus Woodbury, May 26, 1857, to James Tillinghast, whose children are : William Richmond, born April 15, 1858 ; Henry Anthony, born September 15, 1859 ; Theodore Foster, born September 25, 1861 ; Stephen Hopkins, born April 17, 1863, died March 7, 1865 ; Charles Foster, born September 18, 1871 ; Charlotte Lusanne, born November 16, 1872.——George Henry, born June 13, 1835.——Joseph Bowen, born July 16, 1837.——FREDERICK EUGENE, born October 18, 1840 ; married by Rev. Augustus Woodbury, June 5, 1872, to Julia Perkins Adie.

vi. GEORGE, born January 9, 1806; died April 22, 1807.

II. vii. GEORGE WILLIAM, born February 15, 1808.

viii. HELEN ELIZA, born February 23, 1811 ; married September 4, 1834, in Brooklyn, Conn., by Rev. Samuel J. May, to William Lloyd Garrison, of Boston, Mass., where they settled, after various changes, and still live. Their children are :

> George Thompson, born February 13, 1836, in Brooklyn, Conn.——WILLIAM LLOYD, born January 21, 1838, in Boston ; married by Rev. Samuel J. May, September 14, 1864, to Ellen Wright, of Auburn, N. Y., whose children are : Agnes, born June 14, 1866 ; Charles, born June 19, 1868 ; Frank Wright, born October 18, 1871.——WENDELL PHILLIPS, born June 4, 1840, in Cambridgeport, Mass.; married by Rev. William H. Furness, December 6, 1865, to Lucy McKim, of Philadelphia, whose children are : Lloyd McKim, born May 4, 1867 ; Philip McKim, born September 28, 1869.——Charles Follen, born in Cambridgeport, Mass., September 9, 1842 ; died in Boston, April 8, 1849.——HELEN FRANCES, born in Boston, December 16, 1844 ; married by Rev. George Putnam, January 3, 1866, in Roxbury, Mass., to Henry Villard, of Bavaria, Germany. Their children are : Helen Elise, born June 28, 1868 ; Harold Garrison, born December 3, 1869 ; Oswald, born March 13, 1872.——Elizabeth Pease, born in Boston, December 11, 1846 ; died there April 20, 1848.——Francis Jackson, born in Boston, October 29, 1848.

ix. HENRY EGBERT, born July 31, 1814; died in Providence, Tuesday afternoon, January 6, 1837. This favorite son and brother, whose untimely loss was keenly felt by his surviving relatives, was a young man of great beauty of person and character. He commenced business as clerk and bookkeeper for Joseph Rogers, a commission merchant of Providence, dealing principally in cotton. His leisure time and his evenings he spent in improving the condition of the colored population in that city, every family of whom he visited in his benevolent rounds ; and his first public address was to a colored audience. He resided in Providence during the years 1831-34. When not yet nineteen, we find him at Canterbury, Conn., on an errand connected with the Prudence Crandall affair (see Rev. S. J. May's "Recollections of our Anti-Slavery Conflict," pp. 39-72, and "The Life of Arthur Tappan," pp. 152-158). In 1832,

he was solicited by his future brother-in-law, Wm. Lloyd
Garrison, to act as agent for the *Liberator* in Providence,
he being at the same time agent for Mr. May's Unitarian
paper, called the *Christian Monitor and Common People's
Adviser*. During the first visit of George Thompson, the
celebrated English orator and philanthropist, to this country, in 1835, Henry Egbert served as his travelling asso-
ciate and secretary. In March of that year, in fulfilment
of this engagement, he visited New York and Philadelphia,
and also made a pleasant journey up the North River as
far as Albany, on business connected with the *Liberator*.
In July, he accepted an appointment as Secretary and
General Agent of the Massachusetts Anti-Slavery Society
in Boston, and held this position till March, 1836, keeping
the *Liberator's* books. The immediate cause of his retire-
ment and return to Providence was an attack of typhoid
fever, in convalescing from which he took cold and had a
relapse which left him in an enfeebled condition, and an
easy prey to consumption. He sought medical treatment
in various ways in Boston and Providence, and, as usual,
his condition excited alternate hopes and fears. Towards
the last, in Brooklyn, his health "continued quite comfortable" up to his father's death in December, 1836, soon
after which "there appeared a change in his disorder; and
he complied with the urgent request of several friends to
try steaming as a dernier ressort." He left home about ten
days previous to his decease, and never returned. At
Pawtucket, the doctors gave him up, and he went back to
Providence, where he met his fate composedly, being perfectly sensible to the end. During the last sixteen hours,
he could not lie abed, on account of the great distress he
had in breathing. His remains were deposited in the
North Burying Ground, Providence. An obituary notice
appeared in the *Liberator* of Jan. 21, 1837, from the pen of
Mr. Garrison.

The unusual name of *Egbert* naturally suggested to the compiler
of this genealogy some relationship between the famous Judge
Egbert Benson, of New York, and the Rhode Island family. There
is, however, no evidence to show that any existed, the weight of

tradition being in favor of an English derivation for the latter, while Judge Benson was unquestionably of Dutch descent. The naming of young Benson was apparently due to the same cause to which the historian, Mr. Benson J. Lossing, owes his first name, viz., intimacy of the Judge with the father in each case, and nothing more. Mr. George W. Benson remembers the Judge's visits to his father's house in Providence whenever he came on to attend court. He invariably sent his colored servant—a very gentlemanly man—the day before, to say that his master would give himself the pleasure of passing the following day with them, and to add that he should like for dinner a certain kind of blackfish then only found in the bay about Newport. The next morning always the servant came early to the house, took entire control of the kitchen and dining-room, dressed the fish in the peculiar manner best relished by the Judge, and at table waited behind his master's chair. The host followed the fashion of the times in the liberal use of wines.

FOURTH GENERATION.

John Coddington Benson was born in Douglas, Worcester County, Massachusetts, November 3, 1794. He was the youngest son of the family, strong and enduring from childhood, and of quick and retentive memory. He received a good education, and studied physic and surgery with Dr. Thomas Hubbard, of Pomfret, Conn., acquiring some proficiency, and being called upon to assist in some difficult cases of surgery. He left medicine, temporarily as he then expected, to engage in manufacturing, to which he had been invited; but his success was so great that he never resumed his profession. Beginning March 3, 1813, he gave his attention to all the varieties of cotton, woollen, and silk manufacture. He had previously, indeed, at his father's house, helped grow silk and make it into sewing-silk, and is now, perhaps, the oldest American manufacturer living in the branches just named. His operations became very extensive. In 1838, he removed from New England to New Jersey, built a factory in Trenton, which he carried on till 1843, and then relinquished it on account of his health. He removed to Paterson (where he still resides), and carried on both the cotton and silk manufactures with his customary success.

In the large cotton and woollen factory in which he was employed as superintendent in 1813, he introduced a rigid temperance rule, applicable to all the employees, under pain of discharge. At that time, the company who were the proprietors dealt, as was then common, in ardent spirits, both by wholesale and retail, deriving on that side a large profit from sales to their own hands, which they lost on the other from irregular and imperfect work caused by the Saturday night and Sunday excesses in drinking. Mr. Benson persuaded them to abandon this traffic, and may undoubtedly claim the credit of being the first to enforce temperance principles in manufacturing establishments in this country. His mill being in Worcester County, he frequently drove to Boston and back in the same day, transacting his business, and rising after a short rest to spend a long day in the factory without inconvenience. He remembers while in Boston seeing the Gingko tree transplanted to its present place on the Common, an incident which Dr. Holmes has used in his pleasant manner in his "Autocrat of the Breakfast-Table" (p. 324).

Mr. Benson has been twice married : first, to Mary Ann Kempton, January 1, 1828; born August 24, 1808; died September 12, 1862. She was buried in the family lot at Paterson, where a stone marks her grave. By her he had three daughters and one son, as follows :

i. ELIZA ANN, born October 31, 1828. She married Daniel Kempton, jr., of Woonsocket, R. I.

ii. ELECTA CAROLINE CODDINGTON, born September 22, 1834 ; died August 28, 1854. A sweet and estimable character.

iii. GRACE, born September 23, 1837 ; died November 28 of the same year.

iv. JOHN CODDINGTON, born in Trenton, N. J., March 1, 1844;
died the next day.

Mr. Benson married for his second wife Sarah
Augusta Luther, born February 22, 1823. They
have no children.

" **George William Benson** was born in Providence, February 15, 1808. At the age of fifteen he persuaded his father to purchase a farm in Brooklyn, Conn., as already related. Of this, after the family had removed thither, he had the entire management, and subsequently also of the farm of old Moses Brown, in Providence, going back and forth as the interest of each required. At the age of twenty-three he became a partner in the wholesale and retail wool and leather firm of Benson & Chace, whose place of business was 12 Westminster street, Providence. He still continued his management of the two farms. In 1833, the firm-style became Geo. W. Benson & Co. On the death of his father, at the close of 1836, in accordance with a promise made to his mother, he abandoned mercantile life, and returned to Brooklyn, where he became the head of the house. An experience of four years having shown that the farm could not sustain two families, it was sold finally (Feb.-Apr., 1841); and in the fall of that year he removed to Northampton, settling in that portion of it which for a time was known as Bensonville, but (for reasons growing out of the silk interest) was, after he had left it, given the

name of Florence—since become more legiti-
mately famous for its manufacture of sewing-
machines. Here, in company with Messrs.
Samuel L. Hill and J. Conant, he bought a large
tract of four or five hundred acres, intending to
go into the manufacture of sewing-silk ; but, before they had fairly embarked in this business,
they were seized with the communistic fever
then prevalent, and the result was, on April 8,
1842, an organization of ten persons, including
Messrs. Hill and Benson, but not Mr. Conant, as
"The Northampton Association of Education
and Industry." To this body the Northampton
Silk Company sold its land, dwelling-houses,
factory, saw-mill, and water privileges for about
$31,000. The career of this community, which
is remarkable among other American attempts
in the same direction, and which was dissolved
November 1, 1846, is given (from Mr. Benson's
own statements) in Noyes's "History of American Socialisms," pp. 154–160 (Philadelphia : J.
B. Lippincott & Co., 1870). It may be added
here that Mr. Benson was made president of the
Association, and continued in that office to the
end. In spite of wrangling and friction among
the adults, the children's life in these five years
was joyous and to be remembered with pleasure.
They shared fully in the industry of the enterprise by taking the whole care of the silkworms
and the field of mulberries on which they fed :

the boys cultivating the field and helping the girls pull the leaves, and the girls feeding the worms. After all it was found cheaper to import the raw material. The education and amusement of the children were carefully looked after. On the dissolution of the community, Mr. Benson took the brick factory and turned it into a cotton mill, which it still remains, though in other hands. His partners were three men of capital, but having widely different views as to the kind of help to be employed—Mr. Benson aiming to secure the best at good wages—and as to the observance of Sunday, when they objected to the repair of machinery. The result was that Mr. Benson retired, and carried on a silk-mill till the fall of 1850, when he removed with his family to Williamsburgh, Long Island, and undertook the laundry business. In 1855, he removed to New York City, and became a commission broker. Being greatly troubled by his throat, he removed for the sake of the climate to Kansas, in the spring of 1860, settling just outside of Lawrence, where, at this date, he is surrounded by all his family. In the elections of 1869, he was chosen State representative for District No. 136, and in January, 1870, went up to attend the session of the Legislature. In the November election of the same year, he was again chosen to represent Wakarusa township. Mr. Benson early shared his father's views on

the subject of slavery in particular, and of reform
in general ; and both as an officer of societies
and as a public speaker assisted in the abolition
agitation. Though the Northampton community was not founded in accordance with the
doctrines of Fourier, it sent Mr. Benson as one
of its representatives to the first convention
which introduced Fourierism to New England,
and he was made a vice-president (December,
1843–January, 1844, in Boston ; see Noyes, p.
514).

Mr. Benson was married, in Waltham, Mass.,
to Catherine Knapp Stetson, Tuesday, December 10, 1833. She was born May 21, 1809.
Their children were as follows :

i. ANNA ELIZABETH, born in Providence, September 23, 1834 ;
married September 23, 1852, in Williamsburgh, L. I., to Dr.
Edward R. Percy. They have had one child, Charlotte
Helen, born July 17, 1860 ; died in Kansas, January 7, 1870.

ii. HENRY EGBERT, born in Brooklyn, Conn., October 7, 1837.

iii. GEORGE, born in Brooklyn, January 7, 1839.

iv. ELIZA DAVIS, born in Brooklyn, February 24, 1841 ; died
of scarlet fever May 3, 1842.

v. THOMAS DAVIS, born in Northampton, September 1, 1842.

vi. MARY, born in Northampton, October 18, 1843 ; married
June 17, 1863, in Wakarusa township, Kansas, to William
L. G. Soule. They have had two children, Helen, born
November 8, 1865, died November 6, 1867 ; and Emma, born
October 7, 1871.

vii. SARAH, born in Northampton, October 17, 1846 ; married
October 13, 1864, in Wakarusa township, to Horace E.
Stone. They have had one child, Mildred, born May 22,
1865.

APPENDIX.

—————▸◂—————

A.

In the fourteenth volume of *The New England Historical and Genealogical Register* (Boston, 1860), pp. 347, 348, Mr. S. G. Drake has printed part of the contents of a volume discovered and copied by him in the Rolls Office, bound in vellum, containing about three quires of foolscap, with an inscription on the vellum nearly the same as this, which is found inside :

Register of the names
of all ye Passinger wch
Passed from ye Porte of
London for on whole
yeare Endinge at
Xp'mas 1635.

The first entry under this heading is of a vessel which sailed vi Januarii 1634 for St. Christophers and the Barbadoes. Then follows :

17 Februarij 1634.
Theis under written names are to be transported to the Barbadoes imbarqued in ye Hopewell Capten Tho: Wood Mr. bound thither. The passengers have taken the oath of Allegeance and Supremacie.

Among the passengers thus registered was WILLIAM BENSON, aged 28. The barque *Falcon* sailed nearly two years later :

25 decembris 1635.
Theis underwritten names passed in a Catch to the Downes ; and were put aboard the aforesaid shipp Tho: Irish Mr. to the Barbadoes.

Among these passengers was HENRY BENSON, aged 19.

These are the earliest emigrants to America of the name of Benson of whom the compiler has found any mention. Inasmuch as Capt. 'Martin' Benson had property interests in St. Kitt's (see ante p. 17), an attempt was made to have the records of that island consulted, but the persons entrusted with this commission went no further than promises.

B.

Rhode Island Bensons apparently not related to those of Newport.

Providence.—Book of Deeds No. 6, pp. 359, 360 (office of the Town Clerk). JACOB BINSON conveys by warranty deed to Col. Samuel Browne, of "Salem in the County of Essextes in the Province of Massachusetts Bay, for £30 current money," a piece of land containing a small dwelling house and 14 "acres of land by the eighteen foot pole" in that part of the township of Providence "towards Mendon." October 2d, in the 12th "year of the reign of our Sovereign Lord George King of Great Brittan," A.D. 1725.

his
Signed   JACOB I BINSON.
mark

Book of Deeds No. 8, pp. 14, 15. JOB BENSON, of Providence, yeoman, conveys by warranty deed to Isaac Richardson, of Providence, for £20 14s. current money of New England, a piece of land containing 9¼ acres by estimation, more or less, in the township of Providence on the easterly side of the seven-mile line. January, 1728.

June 5, 1795, entered the Port of Providence Ship *Charlotte*, BENSON, from Turk's Island.

Nine Partners.—Some years before the Revolution, JACOB BENSON moved hence to Easton, Washington Co., N. Y., where he lived till 1800, when he moved to Cincinnatus, then in Onondaga Co., N. Y. Before leaving Rhode Island, he had married Mary Meach, by whom he had DANIEL, JUDITH, LUSINA, EDWARD, BILDAD, MARGARET, JOHN, DIDYMUS, and ALEXANDER HAMILTON—all dead (1871). He was wounded in the French War.

JOHN BENSON, his brother, was taken prisoner at Ticonderoga, and carried to Montreal, where he suffered very much. With two companions, he broke jail and made his way home through the woods by the aid of a pocket-compass, amid great hardships. He had a large family.

DANIEL BENSON, son of Jacob, had ten children, of whom only two sons survived in 1871. One of these was

Gen. E. W. BENSON, living at Spencerport, Monroe Co., N. Y. He served in the War of 1812, and was "in the Rebellion loyal." In April, 1871, when he communicated these facts, he had one son, DE WITT S., of the firm of John Mott & Co., New York; one in St. Louis; one in Buffalo, N. Y., at 258 Main Street; and one, GEORGE, in Leavenworth, Kansas, firm of MORSE, BENSON & Co., shoe dealers, 66 Massachusetts Street. Gen. Benson was at that date 83 years old. He states that he has never met any person bearing the name with whom he could trace relationship outside of his father's family.

Glocester.—May 2, 1738, ISAAC BENSON, admitted a freeman (Bartlett, Colonial Records, iv.)

1739, first Tuesday in May, JOHN BENSON admitted a freeman. (*Ibid.*)

1760, first Wednesday in May, ISAAC BENSON admitted a freeman. (*Ibid.*)

By the census of 1774, JOBE BENSON had six children, of whom four were males—two above and two under sixteen; and two females—both over sixteen. By the same census, JOHN BENSON had four children, of whom one was a male, above sixteen; and three females, one above and two under sixteen.

A Capt. John Benston cleared for South Carolina from Newport July 29, 1725; returned November 4, and was again bound out November 12. (Boston *News-Letter*, Aug. 5, 12, Nov. 11, 18.)

C.

MASSACHUSETTS *Bensons.*

Hingham.—JOHN BENSON came from Southampton, 1638, in the *Confidence*, aged 30, with wife Mary, and children JOHN and MARY, under four years old; had grant of land at Hingham that year, says Lincoln, 47. He was of Caversham in Oxfordshire; but both the names of place and person were strangely misspelt in *N. E. Geneal. Reg.* ii. 109. (Savage's Genealogical Dictionary.)

Rochester.—JOHN BENSON, by wife Elizabeth, had MARY, born March 10, 1689 (1688, *Reg.*); SARAH, July 15, 1690; EBENEZER, March 16, 1693; JOHN, June 10, 1696, died soon; JOSEPH and BENJAMIN, twins, March 16, 1697; BENNETT, Sept. 10, 1693; MARTHA, March 5, 1703; JOSHUA and CALEB, twins, Jan. 29, 1705 (1704, *Reg.*); and SAMUEL, March 22, 1707 (1706, *Reg.*) (Savage. The *N. E. Gen. Register* referred to is for 1851, p. 85).

Hull.—[1]JOSEPH BENSON, made freeman in May Court, 1678 (Mass. Records, v. p. 538). Had in Dec., 1675, been a soldier of Johnson's company for the bloody Narragansett fight. (Savage.)

[2]JOSEPH BENSON, son of JOHN of Hull. His first wife was Prince, his second Mary Curtis, of Scituate, 1727, and his third Alice Pickels, 1739. He died in Scituate. (Dean's History of Scituate.) Father of the following:

Scituate.—JOSEPH BENSON, son of the foregoing No. 2, settled in Scituate in 1743. His farm was on the south of Hoop-pole Hill, near Margaret's brook, where his descendants now reside. He married Abiel Stockbridge, 1743. Joseph, his son, was his only child, he having deceased 1745. His widow married John Bryant.

JOSEPH married Susanna, the daughter of Nathaniel Clap, Esq., 1770. He was a useful and worthy man, often employed in the business of the town, and clerk of the second parish for many years. His sons JOHN and JOSEPH are deceased. STEPHEN and ARTEMAS are living in Scituate, and GORHAM in Charleston, S. C. (Dean's History of Scituate, Boston, 1831.)

Plymouth.—June 6, 1682, JOHN BINSON was among those "propounded to take up theire Freedom, if approved" (Colonial Records, vi. p. 87). His name afterwards appears in Nathaniel Morton's list of the freemen of the Colony, 1683-84. (*Ibid.*, viii., p. 203.)

Bridgewater.—JOHN BENSON (from Weymouth perhaps, and son of JOHN of Hull) settled in South Bridgewater, married Elizabeth, daughter probably of Jonathan Washburn [Dec. 4], 1710, and had SUSANNA, BENJAMIN, ELIZABETH, MARY, HANNAH, and JONATHAN ; he died 1770, his will dated the same year, in which it appears Benjamin, Elizabeth, Mary, and Hannah were then dead.—Susannah married Jonathan Cushman, 1736.—Hannah married James Dunbar, jr., 1746, and died about 1757.

2. BENJAMIN (son of John[1]) married Keziah, daughter of Amos Snell, 1745, and had BENJAMIN, an only child, who married Abigail, daughter probably of Nathan Pratt, 1770.—Benjamin, the father, died 1719, and his wife Keziah 1750 ; his will 1748, hers 1749 ; the wife of Benjamin, jr., died 1771.

3. JONATHAN (son of John[1]) married Martha, daughter of Amos Snell, 1740, and had JOHN, 1742 ; EUNICE, 1744 ; MARY, 1745 ; MARTHA, 1749 ; LOIS, 1751 ; JONATHAN, 1752 ; EBENEZER, 1755 ; DAVID, 1756 ; JONAH, 1759 ; he died 1788, of small-pox ; she 1801, aged 84 ; his will, dated 1788, hers 1791.—Eunice married John Harden, 1766.—Mary married Benjamin Hayward, jr., 1767.—Martha married Elisha Waterman of Halifax, 1774.—Lois married Cornelius Washburn, jr.

4. JONATHAN (son of Jonathan[3]) married Lydia, daughter probably of Samuel Harden, 1774, and had JOHN, BETSEY, CYRUS, JONATHAN, and ABIGAIL, and perhaps others ; he died 1802, æt. 50.—John died 1805, æt. 27.—Cyrus married Lydia, daughter of Capt. Simeon Wood, 1806.—Jonathan married Jane, daughter of Jonah Benson, 1820.—Abigail married Samuel Jones, 1811.

5. EBENEZER (son of Jonathan[3]) married Silence, daughter of Nehemiah Packard and widow of Seth Leonard, 1777, and had a daughter, OLIVE, who married Martin Conant, 1797, and had two sons, ASA and HOSEA ; and all went to Jay in Maine.

6. DAVID (son of Jonathan[3]) married Charity, daughter of Seth Hayward, 1780, and had TABITHA, 1781 ; EUNICE, 1782 ; CHARITY, 1784 ; SARAH, 1786 ; DAVID, 1788 ; SETH, 1790 ; BETHIAH, 1793 ; KEZIAH, 1796 ; POLLY, 1798.—Tabitha married Wm. Fuller, 1801.—Eunice married Abner Keith, 1803.—Charity married Ebenezer Cushman, of Kingston, 1805.—Sarah mar-

ried James Pool, jr., about 1808.—Bethiah married Seth Thompson, 1815.—
Keziah married John Atwood Jackson, 1815.—Polly married Ebenezer
Chamberlin, 1820.

7. JONAH (son of Jonathan[3]) married Martha Thompson of Halifax,
1782, and had JONAH, WAITSTILL, PATTY, NAHUM, LUCIA, and JANE.—Jonah
married Chloe Hathaway, 1819.—Waitstill married Benjamin Holmes,
1807.—Patty married Philander Wood, 1813.—Nahum married Chloe Dunbar, 1819.—Lucia married a Drake.—Jane married Jonathan Benson, 1820.
JOHN BENSON married Sarah Williams, 1765.—KEZIAH married Ebenezer Cushman, jr., of Kingston, 1805.—HANNAH married Jabez Waterman of
H., 1785. (Mitchell's History of the Early Settlement of Bridgewater, Boston, 1840.)

Taunton.—JOSEPH BENSON married Deborah Smith, April 17, 1699.
(*N. E. Geneal. Register*, xiii. p. 253.)

Brookline.—BENJAMIN BENSON, of Brookline, is mentioned in the inter-
leaved almanac of Samuel Sewall, jr., April 17, 1724. (*N. E. Geneal. Register*, xvi. p. 65.)

Framingham.—Nero Benson, colored servant of Mr. Swift, married
Dido Dingo, 1731. He was trumpeter in Capt. Clark's Company, 1726, and
a legacy to Ebenezer Robie, 1742. (Barry's History of Framingham, Boston, 1847.) It is not known from what master he derived his surname.

Middleborough.—On the roll of Capt. Job Pierce's company from this
town, which made a secret expedition to Tiverton, R. I., in 1777, being
thirty days on duty, appear the names of privates JOHN BENSON and ISAAC
BENSON. (*N. E. Geneal. Register*, xxii. p. 176.)

Freetown.—This was a Tory town, but Capt. Levi Rounsevill's minute
company marched hence on the alarm on the 19th of April, 1775, twelve
miles, doing three days' duty. Among the privates on the muster-roll was
JACOB BENSON, who afterwards (October, 1775) served under the same commander as a member of the 9th Regiment Continental Army. (*N. E. Geneal.
Register*, xxii. pp. 175, 180.)

Douglas.—Capt. AARON BENSON was (some time prior to 1824) sub-
scriber to the narrative of the voyages of Rev. John Benson (see ante p. 23).

Mendon.—JARED BENSON and JOHN BENSON were subscribers to the
same book.

FRANCIS BENSON was master's mate, and JACOB BENSON quarter-gun-
ner, on board the U. S. frigate *Essex*, Capt. Edward Preble, on her first
voyage, 1800. (Essex Institute *Hist. Coll.*, X., iii. p. 53.)

D.

Maine BENSONS.

Jay.—See ante Bridgewater, Mass., No. 5.

Kittery.—HENRY BENSON, whose wife's name was Quint, went from Kittery to Biddeford before 1750. Several of his children married and settled in Arundel. HENRY married Susan Fletcher; MERCY, Benjamin Littlefield; LUCY, Benjamin Green; LYDIA, Timothy Crawley and James Adams; and OLIVE, Isaac Curtis, Edmund Jeffery, and John Tarbox. Three of the sons remained in Biddeford, and one lived in Kittery. The children of Henry, jr. (of Arundel), were HENRY, married Hannah Huff; LYDIA, James Adams; BETSY (not married); SAMUEL, Mary Huff; JOHN, Abiel Springer; ROBERT, Lydia Stone; JAMES, and one other who died young. (Bradbury's History of Kennebunk Point. 1837.)

Winthrop.—SAMUEL P. BENSON, member of the Maine Historical Society, 1847. See Appendix H below.

E.

NEW HAMPSHIRE *Bensons.*

Portsmouth.—MERCY BENSON married Nathaniel Brown, also of Portsmouth, 1714 (?) (*N. E. Register*, xxiii. p. 270.)

JEMIMA BENSON, of Portsmouth, married John Allixander, of Durham, England, Oct. 7, 1716. (*Ibid.*, p. 393.)

JOHN BENSON married Hannah Brown, also of Portsmouth, June 18, 1724. (*Ibid.*, Jan., 1870, p. 17.)

ANNA BENSON, of Portsmouth, married John Searle, of Luppitt, Devonshire, England, Aug. 31, 1726. (*Ibid.*)

Newington.—JAMES BENSON married Susanna Row, April 8, 1725. (*Ibid.*, xxii. p. 24.)

JOSEPH BENSON married Mary Yeaton, June 1, 1759. (*Ibid.*, p. 156).

F.

VERMONT *Bensons.*

South Royalton.—JAMES BENSON married, about 1816, Sylvia Mason, a descendant of Major John Mason who destroyed the Pequots. (*N. E. Register*, xvii. p. 41.)

G.

NEW YORK *Bensons.*

Easthampton, Long Island.—In David Gardner's history of this town, mention is made of a PETER BENSON who was a schoolmaster there in early times.

New York.—Friday, March 15, 1765, Captain BENSON arrived here from Dover, and last from Plymouth, England. (Boston *News-Letter*, March 28.)

II.

Bensons Graduates of American Colleges.

Columbia, N. Y.—Judge EGBERT BENSON (see ante p. 46), Class of 1765 ; "gradu honorario donatus" by Harvard in 1808. ROBERT BENSON, jr., Class of 1801. EGBERT BENSON, jr., Class of 1807.

Brown, R. I.—MARTIN BENSON, Class of 1806 (see ante p. 20).

Bowdoin, Me.—Hon. SAMUEL PAGE BENSON, Class of 1825 ; president of the college curators in 1870. JOHN BENSON, M.D., Class of 1831. WILLIAM R. BENSON, M.D., Class of 1861.

No person of the name ever graduated at Harvard or at Yale, or, I believe, at Princeton.

I.

Bensons of ENGLAND.

Yorkshire.—JOAN BENSON married Thomas Morton, of Yorkshire, Oct. 18, 1588. (*N. E. Register*, 1850, p. 178.)

Lancaster.—The following extracts are from Fishwick's " History of the Parochial Chapelry of Goosnargh." (London : Trübner & Co. 1871.) Goosnargh is about twenty miles north of Liverpool :

(P. 105.) From the parish registers, which were begun in April, 1639 : " July [1640]. Married was GEORGE BENSON and Katherine Crombleholme the xij. day."

(P. 108.) From the same : "ffebruary [1645 ?]. in templu. Buried was Katherine the wife of George Benson 16th day." "Jan. 1646. in templu. Buried was an infant of Capt. Bensone the xvj. day."

(P. 68.) " Kidsnape Tithe. George Benson—Seaven pence halfe peñy."

Middlesex.—Mr. BRYAN BENSON was first director of the Bank of England for 1722. (Boston *News-Letter*, July 2, 1722.)

Bishop M. BENSON delivered a sermon before the Society for the Propagation of the Gospel in Foreign Parts, Feb. 15, 1739–40, which was printed (London, 1740), and is preserved in the Prince Collection of the Boston Public Library—No. 106.

INDEX OF NAMES.